FOREVER AN EAGLE

EMBRY-RIDDLE AERONAUTICAL UNIVERSITY

~ A PICTORIAL HISTORY ~

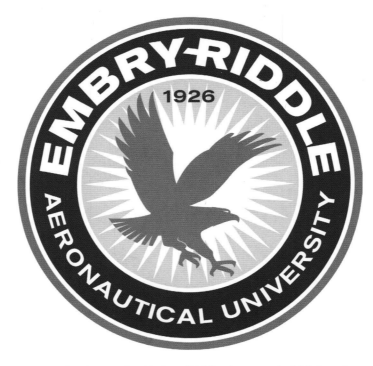

Design and layout: Cyndi Philip, Graphic Designer

Writer: Robert Ross, Assistant Director of Media Relations

Picture Researcher: Kevin Montgomery, University Archivist

Historical Advisor: Stephen Craft, Professor of Social Sciences

     and University Historian

Project Manager: Michele Berg, Executive Director,

     Alumni Association

Proofreader: Sara Withrow, Editor, Alumni Association

Library of Congress Cataloging-in-Publication Data

Forever an eagle : Embry-Riddle Aeronautical University : a pictorial history.
    p. cm.
 Includes bibliographical references and index.
 ISBN 978-1-57864-723-1 (alk. paper)
1. Embry-Riddle Aeronautical University--History. 2. Embry-Riddle Aeronautical University--Pictorial works. I. Embry-Riddle Aeronautical University.
 TL560.2.E49F67 2011
 629.130071′175921--dc23
                        2011040022

Published by:
THE DONNING COMPANY PUBLISHERS
184 Business Park Drive, Suite 206
Virginia Beach, VA 23462

Printed in the United States of America by Walsworth Publishing Company in Marceline, Missouri

CONTENTS

EMBRY-RIDDLE AERONAUTICAL UNIVERSITY LOGOS FROM EARLY YEARS TO PRESENT

the Present

... and beyond

It is with great honor that I introduce this one-of-a-kind pictorial review of the history of Embry-Riddle Aeronautical University. This book is the culmination of years of study, careful preservation and stewardship of the university's expansive archives of photographs and artifacts.

A compilation of Embry-Riddle's rich and illustrious past, this is the first time that these amazing photographs, which document the university's progression from concept to present day, have been showcased together. We expect this book will become a favorite coffee table piece for alumni and friends of the university, as well as history and aviation enthusiasts everywhere.

The Embry-Riddle Company was founded on Dec. 17, 1925 at Lunken Field in Cincinnati, Ohio by barnstormer John Paul Riddle and entrepreneur T. Higbee Embry. The two men came together to start a distributor business for aircraft. From the beginning, they operated a flying school and provided aircraft rides for the adventurous at heart. In 1927, just two years after the formation of The Embry-Riddle Company, the partners were awarded a much sought after airmail contract. Ultimately, it was the education of pilots that proved to be the most durable and impactful of their endeavors.

Today, Embry-Riddle Aeronautical University is still in the business of educating pilots. Its student base and program offerings, however, are much more expansive than they were in the 1920s. The university enrolls more than 34,000 students annually at its three campuses (Daytona Beach, Fla., Prescott, Ariz., and Worldwide at more than 150 locations); it features more than 35 degree programs through the graduate level, including two doctoral programs—with more on the horizon. And, as of May 2011, the university is more than 100,000 alumni strong!

What started as a passion and profit-driven enterprise for two men has evolved into the leading aviation and aerospace university in the world. We commemorate this historic journey; however, the Embry-Riddle story would not be complete without a look at our present and those who brought us here. Special sections are therefore dedicated to celebrating our current programs, facilities and achievements, as well as recognizing our heritage of presidential leadership.

Embry-Riddle's history is a living archive – we continue to grow, plan and progress to meet the needs of our students and the aerospace industry that we serve. I am pleased to share the memories and moments that have made Embry-Riddle what it is today, immortalized now before you in this beautiful pictorial history. I am proud to be President of this institution (since 2005)—to be a part of its past—and its future.

Warmest regards,

John P. Johnson, Ph.D.
President

In 2011, Embry-Riddle celebrated an important milestone – 100,000 graduates since its founding. But for years, the university has been known for the accomplishments of its alumni. Six astronauts, one out of five of the nation's professional pilots, CEOs and top leadership of airlines, aerospace corporations, and technology enterprises, award-winning air traffic controllers, and distinguished scientists. These graduates carry the Embry-Riddle name and reputation forward, creating a network of excellence throughout the world.

Photos clockwise from left: ZANE ROWE, EXECUTIVE VICE PRESIDENT AND CHIEF FINANCIAL OFFICER FOR CONTINENTAL AIRLINES, INC., '91.; ASTRONAUT NICOLE STOTT, '87; USAF THUNDERBIRDS MAJOR AARON JELINEK '01, MAJOR JASON MOORE '00, AND MAJOR J.R. WILLIAMS '01.

Opposite page: 2011 EMBRY-RIDDLE AERONAUTICAL UNIVERSITY GRADUATES CELEBRATE.

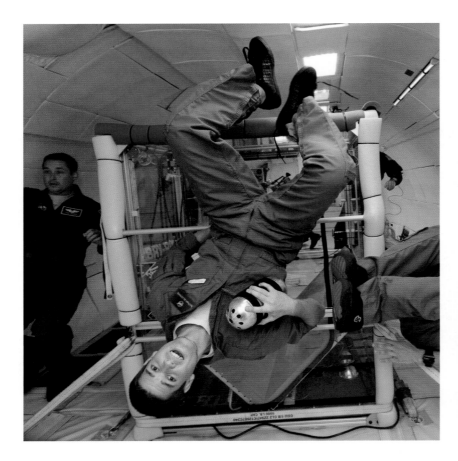

Embry-Riddle research is unique. Its faculty members apply theoretical principles to real-world problems, creating solutions that go to work right away. They are testing new air traffic management systems, designing hybrid automobile engines, clean energy systems, and unmanned aerial and ground vehicles.

Six Embry-Riddle alumni have flown into space as astronauts, one of the nation's highest achievements.

As the U.S. space program moves from the federally funded shuttle program to commercially launched vehicles and access, Embry-Riddle is moving to become a leader in the commercial race for space. Its faculty members are studying space debris hazards, spaceport planning and design, space traffic management, the impact of low orbit radiation on humans, and the development of commercial launch and recovery operations. Others are studying the near-Earth atmosphere, and solar flares.

Photos clockwise from left: Nathan Silvernail floats during a microgravity experiment in the NASA reduced gravity program.; The Stemme glider, a glider that faculty and student researchers fitted with a hybrid motor for the national Green Flight Challenge; Massood Towhidnejad, professor of software engineering, displays a prototype of Gale, the hurricane-sensing UAV his lab has designed.

Opposite page: Embry-Riddle Aeronautical University Astronaut Alumni; Students on the Daytona Beach Campus pause to watch a space shuttle launch.

Previous page: Embry-Riddle's hybrid vehicle entry in the General Motors EcoCAR Challenge takes a test run at Daytona International Speedway.

Susan Still-Kilrain

Daniel Burbank

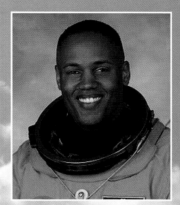
Alvin Drew

Nicole Stott

Ronald Garan, Jr.

Terry Virts, Jr.

Embry-Riddle has built on its aviation foundation. Today the university graduates more engineers than pilots and its undergraduate program in aerospace engineering has been ranked first in the nation for the last 12 consecutive years (2001-2012). Source: *U.S. News and World Report.*

Above photo: STUDENTS DESIGN AND BUILD AN AUTONOMOUSLY CONTROLLED HELICOPTER IN ONE OF THE UNIVERSITY'S UNMANNED AUTONOMOUS SYSTEMS LABORATORIES.

Opposite page: BOTH RESIDENTIAL CAMPUSES HAVE STATE-OF-THE-ART ENGINEERING FACILITIES, INCLUDING THE LEHMAN CENTER IN DAYTONA BEACH.

Embry-Riddle is a leader in the study, improvement, and teaching of flight. The university develops new education and safety models that have elevated the standard in the aviation industry.

The Prescott, Ariz., and Daytona Beach, Fla., campus student flight teams can be counted on to take two of the top three spots, including the national championship, in the annual NIFA SAFECON flight competition.

On its two residential campuses, Embry-Riddle employs nearly 100 training aircraft, fully equipped with ADS-B, a satellite-linked, situational awareness system that soon will be required on all aircraft. The university has used the system since 2003, and helps improve it for the aviation industry. The Prescott Campus also offers rotorcraft pilot programs.

Embry-Riddle also helps test new technology for the FAA's NextGen, an ambitious program to improve the nation's air traffic management system using satellite-linked communications for more precise navigation, and to increase the efficiency and safety of air travel, while and lowering its fuel emissions and costs.

Photos left to right: KRISTEN MCTEE, LEFT, AND KRISTINE ANTHONY REPRESENTING THE PRESCOTT CAMPUS IN THE 2011 AIR RACE CLASSIC; DAYTONA BEACH CAMPUS FLIGHT LINE; PRESCOTT CAMPUS FLIGHT LINE.

Opposite page: EMBRY-RIDDLE AERONAUTICAL UNIVERSITY'S DIAMOND DA42 TWIN STAR AIRCRAFT.

Previous page: AN EMBRY-RIDDLE AIRCRAFT TAKES OFF IN PRESCOTT, ARIZ.

Embry-Riddle's student athletes compete in the National Association of Intercollegiate Athletics in 21 men's and women's sports – baseball, basketball, cross-country, golf, hockey, soccer, tennis, track, volleyball, and wrestling. Its athletes are conference champions in many sports, and the men's soccer team has the highest GPA in the nation.

Photos clockwise from left: BASKETBALL, SOFTBALL, VOLLEYBALL, AND WRESTLING ARE ONLY FOUR OF EMBRY-RIDDLE'S EXCITING INTER-COLLEGIATE SPORTS.

Opposite page: BASEBALLS AND BATTER'S HELMETS AT REST BETWEEN PRACTICES.

Embry-Riddle's athletic programs bring out the best in competitors and spectators alike – spirit, dedication, and bonds that can last a lifetime. The university's student athletes also boast a higher overall GPA than the rest of the student body.

Photos clockwise from left: EMBRY-RIDDLE'S 21 SPORTS INCLUDE TENNIS, TRACK, AND SOCCER.

Opposite page: ERNIE EAGLE STIRS UP CAMPUS SPIRIT DURING ATHLETIC EVENTS.

Self-discipline, rigorous training, the pursuit of excellence, teamwork – these qualities are shared in a special way by Embry-Riddle's ROTC students. The combined enrollment in Air Force, Army, and Navy ROTC is larger than any other university.

Photos clockwise from left: STUDENTS CAN TRAIN TO BE OFFICERS IN THE AIR FORCE, ARMY, OR NAVY AT EMBRY-RIDDLE.

Opposite page: CADETS STAND AT ATTENTION IN THE EVENING SUNLIGHT.

Prescott Campus

Daytona Beach Campus

For nearly 7,000 students, Embry-Riddle's campuses are home away from home. Half of the university's residential students live on campus. Learning also takes place outside the classroom. There are hundreds of student clubs, offering a diverse range of activities, from airport managers to ultimate frisbee. Students work together on projects for class and for clubs. They form friendships and bonds that will continue for the rest of their lives as Embry-Riddle alumni.

Embry-Riddle offers more than 35 degree programs through the graduate level. In 2010 the university introduced its first two Ph.D. programs – in Aviation and in Engineering Physics. Additional doctoral degrees are planned to launch in the near future. At Embry-Riddle, students have more opportunities to assist their professors with research than students do at other universities. They work in laboratories that specialize in airspace management, jet propulsion, aviation operations, flight simulation, air traffic simulation, aircraft accident investigation, laser inferometer gravitational wave observatory, space physics research, high performance vehicles, and other areas of research.

Photos clockwise from left: SOCIAL AND RECREATIONAL OPPORTUNITIES ON CAMPUS ENHANCE THE QUALITY OF STUDENT LIFE.

Opposite page: STUDENTS RELAX OUTSIDE THE BEAUTIFUL STUDENT VILLAGE RESIDENTIAL COMPLEX AT THE DAYTONA BEACH CAMPUS.

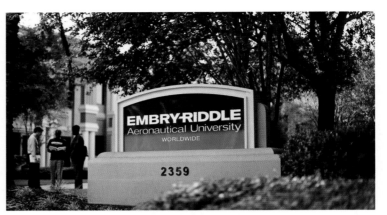

Embry-Riddle Worldwide removes the obstacles to a world-class education for working adults, with coursework offered at more than 150 locations around the globe. Classrooms are located throughout the United States, as well as in Canada, Europe, the Mideast, and Asia. Courses are flexibly scheduled and taught by experts with real-world experience who are leaders in their fields. Embry-Riddle Worldwide also delivers courses online using EagleVision technology, a web-based video conferencing platform.

Photos clockwise from left: EMBRY-RIDDLE'S WORLDWIDE STUDENTS CAN BE FOUND WHEREVER THEY ARE DEPLOYED — STATESIDE, ON A MILITARY BASE, OR IN A WAR ZONE.

Opposite page: WORLDWIDE'S ONLINE TECHNOLOGY ALLOWS STUDENTS TO GET THEIR EDUCATION "ON THE FLY."

In addition to their visibility as successful individuals, many alumni and friends of the university take that extra step to promote Embry-Riddle and career opportunities in aviation and aerospace. One example is Jamail Larkins '07, who earned a bachelor's degree in aviation business administration at the university. In his DreamLaunch Tour, Larkins uses his own life story – flying lessons at age 12, flying solo at 16, and performing in his first aerobatic show at 18 – to inspire school children across America to consider careers in aviation and aerospace. Veteran aerobatic performer Matt Chapman flies the Embry-Riddle Eagle 580, a Mudry CAP, gaining invaluable exposure for the university among millions of air show fans worldwide. Larsen Motorsports performs across the country with a jet dragster that Embry-Riddle students and professors helped design. The vehicle's driver is Marisha Falk '08, '10, who holds a master's in business administration from Embry-Riddle, as well as a bachelor's degree in aeronautical science. Falk also flew for Embry-Riddle in the 2009 Women's Air Race Classic.

Photos clockwise from left: Marisha Falk drives an Embry-Riddle sponsored jet dragster; Jamail Larkins inspires schoolkids across the country with his DreamLaunch Tour.

Opposite page: Matt Chapman's Embry-Riddle sponsored Mudry CAP thrills millions at air shows every year.

Embry-Riddle offers unique opportunities for women seeking the skills and knowledge necessary for rewarding careers in aviation and aerospace. Embry-Riddle has educated women since it started its Flying School in 1926. While female student enrollment has been historically lower than that of males, the number of women completing Embry-Riddle degrees has grown over the years along with the university and its program offerings. Active Women's and Diversity Centers at both residential campuses provide female students many avenues of support, guidance, and collaboration with a variety of programs that empower them to take control of their future success. The Women's Initiative at Embry-Riddle, inaugurated in 2011, further supports female students through mentorship and alumni and student ambassador programs, while enhancing outreach activities for middle and high school-age girls interested in careers in aviation, aerospace maintenance and engineering, mathematics, and business.

Photos clockwise from left and opposite page: EMBRY-RIDDLE'S WOMEN'S AND DIVERSITY CENTERS GIVE STUDENTS A COMFORTABLE PLACE TO GATHER AND SUPPORT UNIVERSITY ACTIVITIES SUCH AS BUILDING AND RACING A BAJA CAR, CONDUCTING RESEARCH, AND MORE.

Just as education is a human activity, always dynamic and in motion, the spaces where it is carried out must also expand and evolve. Embry-Riddle continually seeks to provide its students, faculty, and staff with the best teaching and research facilities possible. On the university's residential campuses, there seems always to be projects underway and on the drawing board to upgrade existing structures and to build new state-of-the-art facilities.

Above photo: STUDENTS PREPARE FOR FLIGHTS IN THE FLIGHT OPERATION CENTER OF THE JAMES HAGEDORN AVIATION COMPLEX, WHICH OPENED IN 2011 AT THE DAYTONA BEACH CAMPUS.

Opposite page: A VIEW OF EMBRY-RIDDLE'S FLIGHT LINE FROM THE HANGAR IN THE HAGEDORN AVIATION COMPLEX.

Previous page: FLIGHT INSTRUCTORS AND AVIATION MAINTENANCE STAFF POSE AT THE JAMES HAGEDORN AVIATION COMPLEX IN 2011.

Embry-Riddle's campuses are as warm and welcoming as they are high-tech and innovative. Small class sizes encourage maximum student-faculty interaction, promoting an advanced learning environment; while residential facilities, situated on campus, create a strong sense of community and provide easy access for students to classes, laboratories and extracurricular activities.

Photos clockwise from left: James Henderson Welcome and Administration Center at the Daytona Beach Campus; Athletic complex at Daytona Beach; The Aerospace Experimentation and Fabrication Building at Prescott .

Opposite page: The Academic Complex at the Prescott Campus is marked by its stunning architechtural design.

Following page: An aerial view of the James Hagedorn Aviation Complex, Daytona Beach Campus.

the Early Years

1920s and 1930s

The Embry-Riddle Aeronautical University of today is the product of a long and prestigious history. Embry-Riddle got its start after barnstormer John Paul Riddle met entrepreneur T. Higbee Embry and in 1925 the two partnered to create the Embry-Riddle Company at Lunken Field in Cincinnati. In the beginning the company taught the adventurous to fly as the Embry-Riddle Flying School. In addition, the company sold aircraft rides and became a distributor for WACO, Fairchild, and Monocoupe aircraft.

They quickly expanded to include an aerial advertising service and even established one of the first travel agencies to promote flying. By 1927, the company had started flying passengers and cargo between Louisville, Cleveland, and Cincinnati. Later that year, the Embry-Riddle Company was awarded a sought-after air mail contract and became the first regular air mail carrier in Cincinnati, making the city one of the first in the country to have direct air mail service.

By 1928, interest in aviation was increasing and the Embry-Riddle Flying School grew significantly. The company established the Air Pilots, a "flying basketball team," which was the first all-pilot sport team in the country and the first team to fly to their out-of-town games – piloting the school's aircraft. In some cases, the team even flew in formation to their games.

In 1929, Embry-Riddle was one of the first five flying schools in the country to be certified under the Department of Commerce's new Air Commerce Act. However, later that year, the Embry-Riddle Company merged with the newly-formed Aviation Corporation (AVCO), an alliance that came with a price. Although Embry-Riddle's airline and cargo routes remained prosperous, the company no longer sold aircraft, and in 1930 AVCO closed Embry-Riddle's flying school. A year later, Embry left the company and retired to California. In 1932, AVCO moved its Embry-Riddle Division to St. Louis where it was merged into a new division called American Airways, and the original Embry-Riddle Company was no more.

Flight instruction by the Embry-Riddle Flying School included aerodynamics, aerial navigation, motor overhaul and repair, meteorology, plane inspection and maintenance, and air rules and regulations. In 1927, parachute jumping was added to the curriculum. By the close of that year, 80 students had received certificates.

The Embry-Riddle Flying School was a pioneer in its development of a standardized curriculum. In 1929, the school instituted a 30-course program that prepared students to get a transport pilot's license. The first class had 35 students, including two women.

Above photo: EMBRY-RIDDLE'S FIRST HEADQUARTERS AT LUNKEN FIELD IN CINCINNATI, OHIO.

Opposite page: JOHN PAUL RIDDLE FLYING OVER CINCINNATI (1926).

Previous page: FORD TRI-MOTOR AIRCRAFT WAS ONE OF THE AIRPLANES FLOWN BY EMBRY-RIDDLE STUDENTS AND EMPLOYEES (1928).

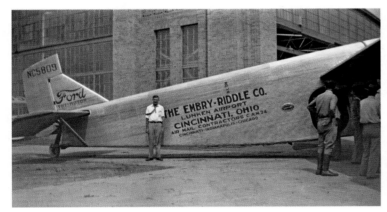

Seeing themselves as "missionaries for this new and faster form of transportation," John Paul Riddle and T. Higbee Embry did all they could to promote aviation – and benefit from it. From their offices at Lunken Airfield in Cincinnati, Ohio, they sold WACO, Fairfield, and Monocoupe airplanes. An early ad slogan: "If it's flying, we do it. If it's airplanes, we have them."

Photos clockwise from left: EMBRY-RIDDLE WAS ONE OF THE NATION'S LARGEST WACO DEALERS; AN EARLY EMBRY-RIDDLE HANGAR; ONE OF THE FIRST ENCLOSED-COCKPIT PLANES IN THE EMBRY-RIDDLE FLEET, A FORD TRI-MOTOR.

Opposite page: HARRY SHERWIN, JOHN PAUL RIDDLE, AND POWELL CROSSLEY, PRESIDENT OF CROSSLEY RADIO CO.

Previous page: POSING BEHIND A WACO AIRPLANE, LEFT TO RIGHT, ARE JOHN PAUL RIDDLE, RICHARD BLYTHE, T. H. EMBRY, CHARLIE MYERS, JOHN WOODS, AND HARRY SHERWIN.

Embry-Riddle hired the best people and John Paul Riddle used his personal charm and engaging personality to befriend well-placed people who could help the up-and-coming enterprise.

Photos clockwise from left: T. HIGBEE EMBRY; A GROUP OF EMBRY-RIDDLE EMPLOYEES; EMBRY AND FIVE EMPLOYEES.

Opposite page: JOHN PAUL RIDDLE IN THE COCKPIT.

John Paul Riddle
Cincinnati
1923-24

Embry and Riddle knew that the aviation industry – and their company – would prosper if more people learned to become pilots. Their flying school included a strong emphasis on safety. In an era when airplanes and landing strips were as rudimentary as the industry itself, pilots had to be prepared for anything.

Above photo: A PARACHUTE JUMP OVER LUNKEN FIELD.

Opposite page: FLIGHT INSTRUCTOR HAROLD MATHNY PREPARES FOR A PARACHUTE JUMP, REQUIRED TRAINING FOR ALL EMBRY-RIDDLE EMPLOYEES.

As exciting as aviation was in the early years – and remains today – it was fraught with risks that required pilots to stay alert, safety-conscious, and fit. Embry-Riddle promoted recreation as "necessary in the modern flying school," in the belief that it enabled students to "develop quick judgment, a cool and calculating temperament, and perfect coordination between decision and action." It was also fun. Recreation options for students included basketball, baseball, tennis, archery, badminton, fencing, and horseshoe pitching.

Above photo: EMBRY-RIDDLE'S BASKETBALL SQUAD PILOTED THE COMPANY'S PLANES TO AWAY GAMES.

Opposite page: AN EMBRY-RIDDLE WRECKER HAULS AWAY A WACO WITH A BROKEN WHEEL. LANDING STRIPS WERE OFTEN GRASSY, RUTTED FIELDS.

Previous page: A FLAMINGO PRODUCED BY THE ALL-METAL AIRCRAFT CO., A NEIGHBOR OF EMBRY-RIDDLE AT LUNKEN FIELD. FLIGHT STUDENTS WENT THERE TO LEARN HOW AIRPLANES WERE MADE.

Above photo: Air mail pilots

On Dec. 17, 1927, Embry-Riddle began to fly U.S. cargo air mail route 24 between Cincinnati and Chicago. Winning a contract to fly U.S. mail between Cincinnati and Chicago gave Embry-Riddle an important source of revenue. It also led to growing pains, acquisition by the Aviation Corporation (AVCO), and a period of transition that set Embry-Riddle on the path to its future as a university.

Above photo: Air mail pilots

Opposite page: Loading air mail onto an Embry-Riddle plane.

Previous page: An air mail WACO plane on a snow-covered landing field. The plane had enough room for one paying passenger. Every flight paid for itself.

Embry-Riddle Reborn

1940s and 1950s

Shortly after the Embry-Riddle Company merged with AVCO in 1929, T. Higbee Embry and John Paul Riddle went their separate ways. Embry moved to Los Angeles in 1931, where he lived the rest of his life. Riddle left in 1932 and moved to south Florida, where he started several airplane businesses, including a charter service that flew passengers to the Caribbean on seaplanes.

By 1939, he was ready to rebuild a flight school. With financing from Miami attorney John McKay, he reopened the Embry-Riddle Company in Miami with two seaplanes, a flight instructor, and a maintenance technician. A year later, the company had a contract to train pilots for the University of Miami as part of the nation's new Civilian Pilot Training Program. The school also opened a Technical Division to teach aeronautical engineering and airplane maintenance, housed in the former Fritz Hotel. By May 1941, 250 students had graduated with private and commercial pilot licenses.

That same year, the U.S. Army Air Corps called with a contract to train several hundred military pilots. As the Riddle Aeronautical Institute, the school quickly built new facilities at the old Carlstrom and Dorr airfields in Arcadia, Fla., converting them into what was described at the time as "the largest non-military-operated flight training center in the United States."

Between 1939 and 1941, Embry-Riddle had grown from a tiny seaplane base in Miami to a school with six divisions at several airfields, 24 aircraft, 96 Stearman trainers loaned by the Army, 87 flight instructors, and 400 employees.

World War II proved a golden opportunity for the school, which trained thousands of war-time American, British, French, Brazilian and other South American cadets to fly and maintain aircraft. In 1941, as part of the Lend-Lease Act, Embry-Riddle was asked by General Henry "Hap" Arnold to train British pilots, and the British Flying Training School No. 5 was established. British cadets trained there alongside their American counterparts for several months at Carlstrom Field, and then at Riddle Field near Clewiston, where 7,000 cadets were trained.

In late 1943, at the request of Brazil's Air Minister, Embry-Riddle established a separate school in Sao Paulo to provide technical instruction to Brazilian cadets. By early 1944, the Escola Tecnica de Aviacao had basic, aircraft, engines and instrument departments.

At the height of the war, Embry-Riddle was the largest privately-operated flight school in the world and had trained 26,000 people, military and civilian, American and foreign. However, as the war drew to a close, the aviation training boom contracted, and so did Embry-Riddle. In September 1944, John McKay bought out John Paul Riddle's interests in Embry-Riddle, and Riddle began pursuing his activities in Brazil on a full-time basis.

After Embry-Riddle was merged into AVCO, T. Higbee Embry retired to California and John Paul Riddle moved to south Florida, where he started several airplane businesses, including a charter service that flew passengers to the Caribbean on seaplanes. By 1939, he was ready to rebuild a flight school, and with financing from attorney John McKay, he reopened the Embry-Riddle Co. in Miami with two seaplanes, a flight instructor, and a maintenance technician.

Above photo: : SEVERAL WOMEN WORKED AS FLIGHT INSTRUCTORS AT THE SEAPLANE BASE AND CHAPMAN FIELD.

Opposite page: : THE EMBRY-RIDDLE CO. SEAPLANE OPERATION IN MIAMI.

Embry-Riddle understood the need for mechanics, and its Technical Division grew quickly. In late 1940, the school needed more space, so it acquired the unoccupied former Fritz Hotel in Miami, renaming it as the Aviation Building. There students learned airplane maintenance and aeronautical engineering, or took specialized courses in welding, sheet metal, radio, and electricity. In less than two years, the school needed space again to train U.S. Army Air Force enlisted men as engine welders, mechanics, electricians, and sheet metal workers, so it occupied the former Coral Gables Coliseum, once renowned as a boxing arena and ice skating rink.

Above photo: EMBRY-RIDDLE'S TECHNICAL DIVISION OCCUPIED THE FORMER CORAL GABLES COLISEUM.

Opposite page: STUDENTS CHANGING CLASSES AT EMBRY-RIDDLE'S AVIATION BUILDING, WHICH HOUSED WORKSHOPS AND CLASSROOMS FOR THE AIRFRAME AND POWERPLANT MECHANICS PROGRAM.

Previous page: INSIDE THE FORMER CORAL GABLES COLISEUM, STUDENTS LEARNED AIRCRAFT MAINTENANCE.

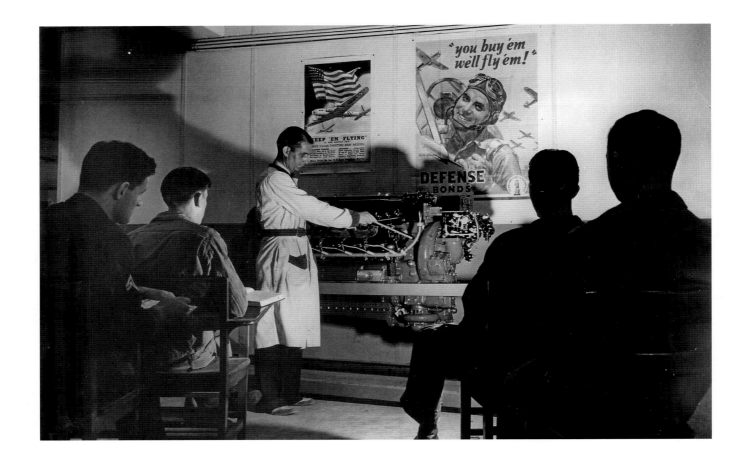

In 1940, Embry-Riddle had a contract to train pilots for the University of Miami as part of the nation's new Civilian Pilot Training Program. The school also opened a Technical Division to teach aeronautical engineering and airplane maintenance, housed in the former Fritz Hotel. By May 1941, 250 students graduated with private and commercial pilot licenses.

Above photo: THE ALLISON ENGINE DEMONSTRATION ROOM.

Opposite page: A SHEET METAL WORKSHOP.

Previous page: THE FORMER FRITZ HOTEL IN MIAMI WAS EMBRY-RIDDLE HEADQUARTERS FROM 1940-1965. IT HOUSED CLASSROOMS, WORKSHOPS, A LIBRARY, AND CAFETERIA.

In 1923, John Paul Riddle was a young flight cadet at Carlstrom Field in Florida. Two decades later, as head of the largest flight school in America, he acquired the airfield where he learned to fly and revitalized it as part of a massive effort to train U.S. and British aviators for World War II.

Photos clockwise from left: JOHN PAUL RIDDLE CHECKING ON CONSTRUCTION OF EMBRY-RIDDLE FACILITIES AT A REVITALIZED CARLSTROM FIELD IN 1941; THE FITNESS PROGRAM INCLUDED CALISTHENICS, TENNIS, AND SWIMMING; GROUND SCHOOL INSTRUCTION AT CARLSTROM.

Opposite page: CADETS SIGNING IN AT THE FLIGHT LINE.

Previous page: A TRADITIONAL PLUNGE IN THE SWIMMING POOL FOLLOWED EACH CADET'S FIRST SOLO FLIGHT.

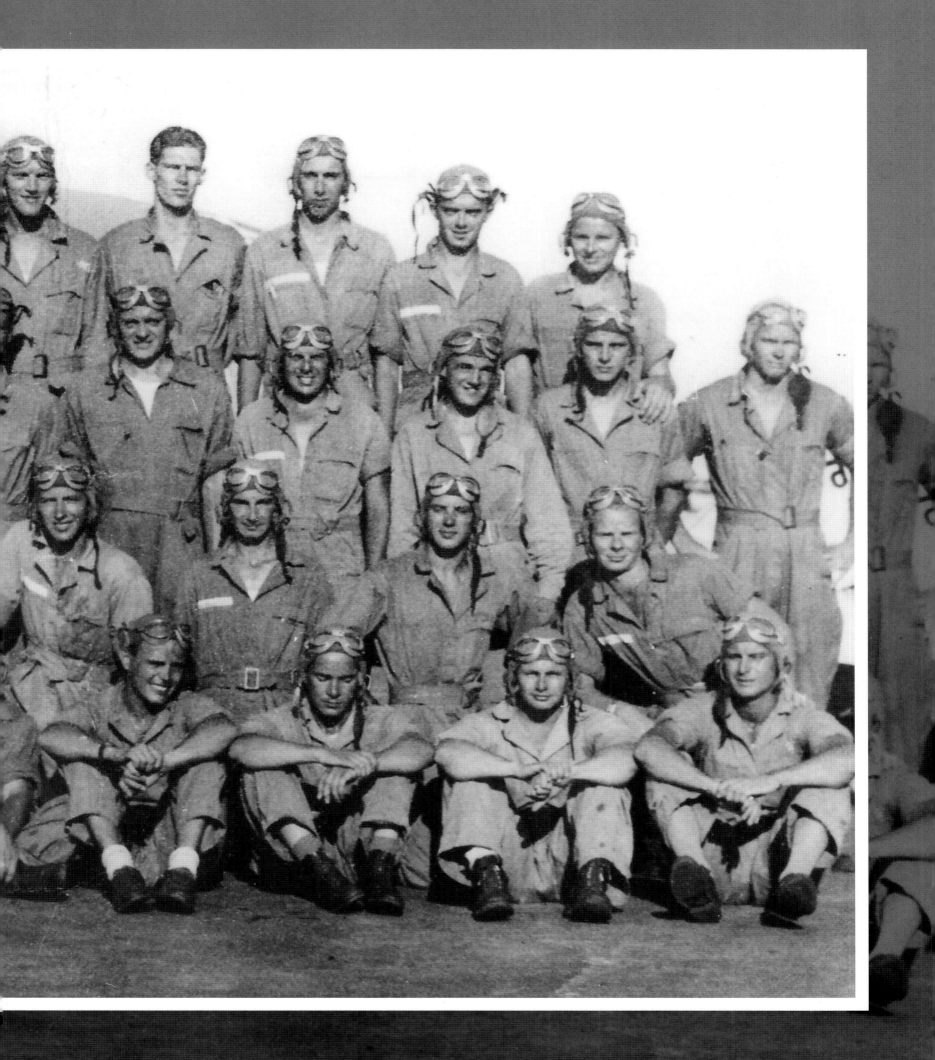

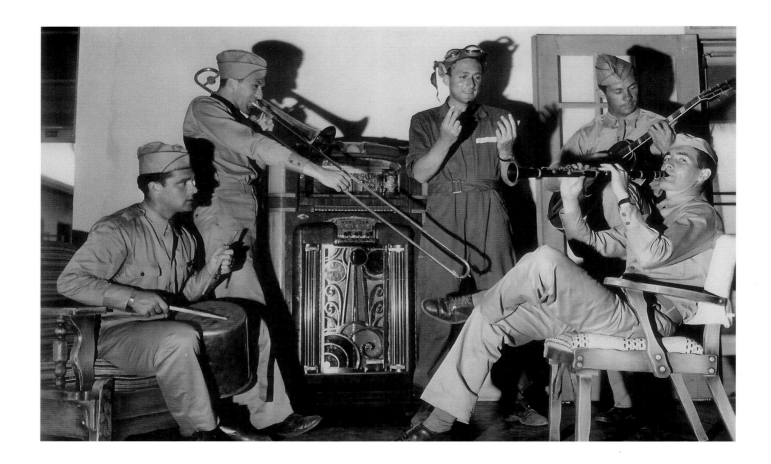

In 1940, the U.S. Army Air Corps contracted with Embry-Riddle Aeronautical Institute to train military pilots. The school quickly built new facilities at the old Carlstrom and Dorr airfields in Arcadia, Fla., converting them into what was described as "the largest non-military-operated flight training center in the United States." During World War II, the school trained 26,000 people, American and foreign, to fly and maintain aircraft at Carlstrom, Dorr, and other airfields in Florida. At the height of the war, Embry-Riddle was the largest privately-operated flight school in the world.

Above photo: CADETS HAVING A JAZZ JAM SESSION AT DORR, LEFT TO RIGHT: A.P. SIEGFRIED, KENNETH H. PROPST, JUSTIN I. FEDERMAN, WILLARD B. GRACE, AND PAUL J. QUIGLEY.

Opposite page: CADETS IN THE READING ROOM AT DORR.

Previous page: A GROUP OF CADETS FROM THE CLASS OF 1943 AT DORR FIELD.

Women played a crucial role in keeping Embry-Riddle in operation during World War II, when fewer men remained on the home front. At Chapman Field, approximately 10 women were flight instructors, including Katherine Kniesche, who had been one of few U.S. female flight instructors before the war. She did her part because she wanted "to get this war over with, so people can get back to flying for fun again." Other women performed such duties as chief dispatchers, radio and drafting instructors, and instrument and engine assemblers.

Above photo: A FEMALE FLIGHT INSTRUCTOR WITH FIVE NAVAL AVIATOR CADETS SHE TAUGHT AT CHAPMAN FIELD.

Opposite page: INSTRUCTORS AND CADETS AT CHAPMAN FIELD IN THE LATE 1940S.

In 1941, as part of the Lend-Lease Act, Embry-Riddle was asked by General Henry "Hap" Arnold to train British pilots, and the British Flying Training School No. 5 was established. British cadets trained alongside their American counterparts for several months at Carlstrom Field and then at Riddle Field near Clewiston, where 7,000 cadets were trained.

Above photo: THESE WOMEN DELIVERED MESSAGES THROUGHOUT THE WIDESPREAD AIRFIELD AT UNION CITY.

Opposite page: AERIAL VIEW OF EMBRY-RIDDLE FIELD AT UNION CITY, TENN.

Previous page: THE EMBRY-RIDDLE FIELD AT UNION CITY, TENN.

In late 1943, Brazil's Air Minister asked Embry-Riddle to establish a school in Sao Paulo to provide technical instruction to Brazilian cadets. By early 1944, the new school, Escola Tecnica de Aviacao, had basic, aircraft, engines and instrument departments.

Above photo: FIRST LADY ELEANOR ROOSEVELT PAID A VISIT TO EMBRY-RIDDLE'S TRAINING FACILITIES IN BRAZIL IN 1944.

Opposite page: STUDENTS LEARNED HOW TO OVERHAUL AIRCRAFT ENGINES AT ESCOLA TECNICA DE AVIACAO.

Previous page: EMBRY-RIDDLE TRAINED 7,000 BRITISH AVIATORS DURING WORLD WAR II AT CARLSTROM AND RIDDLE (CLEWISTON) AIRFIELDS.

As World War II drew to a close, the aviation training boom contracted, and so did Embry-Riddle. In September 1944, John McKay bought out John Paul Riddle's interests in Embry-Riddle, and Riddle pursued his activities in Brazil.

Above photos left to right: ISABEL MCKAY; STUDENTS IN A BASIC ENGINES CLASS IN 1959.

Opposite page: STUDENTS EXAMINE A JET ENGINE FROM A CAPTURED WWII GERMAN AIRPLANE, CIRCA 1950.

Previous page: UPON THE DEATH OF HER HUSBAND JOHN MCKAY IN 1951, ISABEL MCKAY BECAME EMBRY-RIDDLE'S PRESIDENT, AND SERVED UNTIL 1963. SHE WAS WELL LIKED BY THE STUDENTS.

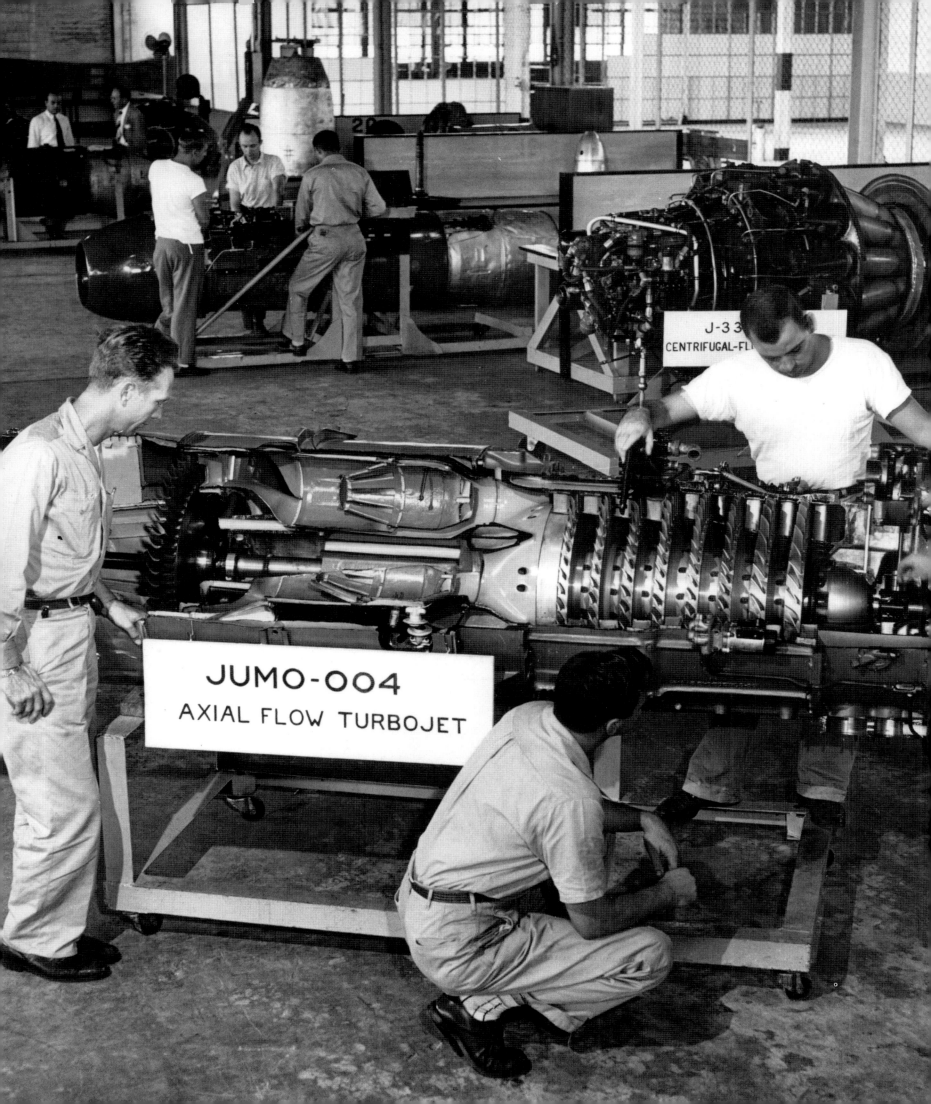

JUMO-004
AXIAL FLOW TURBOJET

J-3 3
CENTRIFUGAL-FL

Embry-Riddle conducted flight training for civilians for several years at Tamiami and Opa Locka airports in Miami.

Above photo: PIPER CUBS AND OTHER EMBRY-RIDDLE TRAINER AIRPLANES AT OPA LOCKA AIRFIELD.

Opposite page: A BEECH 18 BEING FUELED AT EMBRY-RIDDLE'S TAMIAMI FLIGHT LINE IN 1960.

From 1941 until the end of World War II, Embry-Riddle employed renowned photojournalist Charles Ebbets to document the training of U.S. and British Royal Air Force pilots in Florida. Ebbets, whose work had been published in major newspapers including the New York Times when he joined Embry-Riddle, is most famous for his photo "Lunchtime atop a Skyscraper" (1932) that showed 11 construction workers eating lunch on a steel beam suspended hundreds of feet above Manhattan.

T. Higbee Embry and John Paul Riddle

On Dec. 17, 1925, barnstormer John Paul Riddle and entrepreneur T. Higbee Embry founded the Embry-Riddle Company at Lunken Airport in Cincinnati, Ohio. The following spring, they opened the Embry-Riddle School of Aviation.

They began with a simple plan to train airplane pilots in a thorough, efficient manner and to capitalize on a booming interest in flying. Their success flying U.S. mail led to their acquisition in 1929 by the Aviation Corporation (AVCO), which was adding several other fledgling air carriers serving much of the nation. With their company gone, Embry left AVCO and gave up aviation and Riddle moved to south Florida, where he started several airplane businesses during the next decade.

In 1939, Riddle and attorney John McKay reopened the Embry-Riddle Company in Miami as a small seaplane operation. The company quickly sprung to life, taking on contracts to train pilots for the new Civilian Pilot Training Program and teaching aeronautical engineering and airplane maintenance. Soon the Riddle Aeronautical Institute was training hundreds of pilots for the U.S. Army Air Corps at Carlstrom and Dorr airfields in Arcadia, Fla.

When World War II erupted, Allied nations sent more than 25,000 young men to Embry-Riddle's Florida centers to become pilots and aviation technicians. Embry-Riddle also established an aviation school in Sao Paulo, Brazil.

In 1944, McKay bought out Riddle's interests in the school, and Riddle pursued his activities in Brazil. After leaving the school he founded, John Paul Riddle formed Riddle Airlines in Miami, serving as president until he sold the company in 1964. He remained keenly interested in the university's growth and made several visits in his later years to speak to Embry-Riddle students.

John McKay

From 1944-1951, John McKay continued Embry-Riddle's training of pilots and aircraft mechanics. In the years following World War II, the school saw an increase in students, thanks to the GI Bill. After a hurricane caused extensive damage to Embry-Riddle's training aircraft and facilities, McKay put the school back on course when, three days after the storm, he restarted flight operations at Chapman Air Field. He later moved many of the school's operations to a former naval airfield in Opa-Locka, near Miami. The Korean War brought a call for Embry-Riddle to train mechanics for the U.S. Air Force, but when the U.S. Navy reclaimed the Opa-Locka airfield, the school once again had to move the flight line to Tamiami Airport.

Isabel McKay

When John McKay died in 1951, Isabel McKay took over as president, serving in that role until 1962. Under her leadership, the school, renamed Embry-Riddle Aeronautical Institute, expanded its curriculum in aircraft maintenance, drafting, and engineering, and partnered with the University of Miami to allow students to receive a four-year degree in business. Her expansion of the school's flight operations made Tamiami Airport the nation's third most active controlled airfield. Her reorganization of the school as a non-profit organization made it eligible for federal student loans and donations from corporations and government agencies. She increased extracurricular activities and clubs on campus and was very well liked by students.

Jack Hunt

Embry-Riddle's next president, from 1963-1984, was Jack Hunt. In 1965, Hunt consolidated Embry-Riddle's flight and technical training programs in one location by moving the school from Miami to Daytona Beach, Fla. The relocation signaled the revitalization of Embry-Riddle and the start of its odyssey to world-class status in aviation higher education. In 1968, Embry-Riddle was accredited as a university by the Commission on Colleges of the Southern Association of Colleges and Schools, and in 1970 changed its name to reflect its new status. Also in 1970 centers were established at U.S. military aviation bases to serve the educational needs of military personnel, the birth of today's Embry-Riddle Worldwide. In 1978, Embry-Riddle opened a second residential campus in Prescott, Ariz., on the 511-acre site of a former college.

1925   1945 1951   1963

Kenneth Tallman

Continuing Jack Hunt's legacy was Kenneth Tallman, who served as Embry-Riddle's president from 1984-1989, following a distinguished military career that included service as superintendent of the U.S. Air Force Academy. Under Tallman's leadership, a school of graduate studies and the electrical engineering degree program were introduced. He led the university into research with the addition of the engineering physics degree program and developed stronger ties with the aviation and aerospace industries.

John Johnson

John Johnson assumed the presidency of Embry-Riddle in 2006 after serving as interim president and provost and chief academic officer. Under his leadership, the university has expanded its research activity and launched its first Ph.D. degree programs, in aviation and engineering physics. Other initiatives include new degree programs in computational mathematics, homeland security, project management, transportation, and mechanical engineering. He is also developing a global strategy to take Embry-Riddle's aviation and aerospace education overseas, most recently by opening locations in Singapore and Berlin. Working with the FAA and industry leaders, Johnson has positioned the university as one of the nation's leaders in the development of next-generation air traffic management technology.

George Ebbs

George Ebbs led the university from 1998-2005. During his tenure, Ebbs introduced a new graduate degree program in safety science, as well as new undergraduate programs in computer science, global security and intelligence studies, software engineering, and space physics. Ebbs also initiated aviation-training contracts with the U.S. military in Europe, Kirtland Air Force Base in Albuquerque, N.M., and the U.S. Air Force Academy.

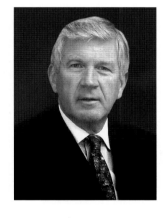

Steve Sliwa

Steve Sliwa led the university from 1991-1998. He is best known for creating an entrepreneurial environment and forming strategic partnerships with corporations. These ventures included agreements with FlightSafety International, Cessna Aircraft Co., IBM, and the Aircraft Owners and Pilots Association. He also spearheaded a $100 million capital expansion program that included an $11.5 million congressional line-item appropriation. New academic and research programs were also created to respond to changes in the industry.

On the residential campuses, Johnson has spearheaded new construction to improve research, teaching, and student life. On the Daytona Beach Campus, new facilities include the College of Business building, the James Hagedorn Aviation Complex, the Jim Henderson Administration and Welcome Center, Apollo Hall student residences, Tine Davis Fitness Center, and expansion of athletic facilities. On the Prescott Campus, new construction includes the Christine and Steven Udvar-Hazy Library, the Fred and Fay Haas Interfaith Chapel, the Robertson Aviation Safety Center II, and improvements in dining and services facilities. Future plans call for the construction of a College of Arts and Sciences Building and a Aerospace Research and Technology Park in Daytona Beach.

| 1984 | 1991 | 1998 | 2006 |

a New Kind *of* University

1960s through Present

In the immediate postwar years, Embry-Riddle's perseverance and ingenuity allowed it to survive and remain on the cutting edge of aviation education. By the early 1960s, the school was expanding once again and quickly outgrew its facilities in Miami. Embry-Riddle's newly-elected president, Jack R. Hunt, made the decision to move the school out of Miami and started a search for a new home.

Hunt chose Daytona Beach because of the support of the local community and because it was located near the Kennedy Space Center and the space industry, which he saw as crucial to the school's future.

In 1965, Embry-Riddle made its historic move from Miami to Daytona Beach in "Operation Bootstrap." The move saw a contingent of volunteers from the community as well as faculty members and students driving trucks loaded with furniture, equipment, tools, and other supplies up the Florida coast from Miami to Daytona Beach in one weekend.

Accreditation as a full-service university soon followed and, in 1970, the school had a new name, Embry-Riddle Aeronautical University. That same year, the university began offering courses to personnel at military installations in the United States and Europe. Today, Embry-Riddle Worldwide offers degree programs to working adults at over 150 sites around the world, and through online study. In 1978, the school expanded once again when it opened a second residential campus in Prescott, Ariz.

When Jack Hunt died in 1984, Embry-Riddle appointed Kenneth Tallman as president. Tallman added degrees in avionics technology, business administration, electrical engineering, engineering physics, and a master's in aeronautical engineering. On the Daytona Beach Campus, he built a library and administration building and, in Prescott a student cafeteria, new dormitories, and an expanded library.

In 1991, Embry-Riddle appointed Steve Sliwa as its new president. Sliwa spearheaded new construction in Daytona Beach that added more space for research, flight operations, engineering, and classes, and living space for 1,000 students. He also added seven new undergraduate degrees and three new master's programs.

From 1998 to 2005, George Ebbs served as president. Ebbs tested a number of programs to deliver flight training in contracts with the civil aviation authorities of Saudi Arabia and Turkey and to the U.S. Air Force Academy. The College of Aviation received a new building, and degree programs in air traffic management, meteorology, global security and intelligence studies, and safety science were added.

In 2006, John Johnson assumed the presidency of Embry-Riddle after serving as interim president and provost and chief academic officer. Under his leadership, the university has expanded its research activity and launched its first Ph.D. degree programs – in aviation and engineering physics. He is also developing a global strategy to take Embry-Riddle's education overseas into regions where aviation and aerospace are experiencing dramatic growth. He most recently opened a Singapore location. Working with the FAA and industry leaders, Johnson has positioned the university as one of the nation's leaders in the development of next-generation air traffic management technology.

When Embry-Riddle's new president, Jack Hunt, decided to move the university, the school was operating in several locations throughout Miami. Relocation would allow the school to consolidate its resources, expand to accommodate more students, and give it the campus it would need for accreditation as a university. The move to Daytona Beach in 1965, dubbed "Operation Bootstrap," lasted 19 days and benefitted from the sweat of volunteers and the pluck of pioneers – those who envisioned a new beginning for Embry-Riddle.

Above photos left to right: Jack Hunt served as president from 1963 to 1984, ushering in a new era for Embry-Riddle; Many Daytona Beach area businesses and organizations pitched in with manpower and vehicles to help move Embry-Riddle to its new home, including the Jaycees, Cunningham Oil, BM Beach and Sons General Contractors, and *(opposite page)* the News-Journal.

Previous page: A caravan of trucks and moving vans driven by volunteers makes its way up the Florida coastline from Miami to Daytona Beach to establish Embry-Riddle's new home.

Embry-Riddle
AERONAUTICAL UNIVERSITY
32
skyhawk II
N20931

Embry-Riddle's first academic year at its new campus was difficult, but marked by progress as the school scrambled to acquire temporary buildings for a library, student center, and classrooms. Eventually, financing was found to build a permanent student center and expand the flight line.

Above photo: A VIEW INSIDE THE FIRST LIBRARY ON THE DAYTONA BEACH CAMPUS, CIRCA 1968.

Opposite page: BRIG. GEN. BILL SPRUANCE, CHAIRMAN OF THE BOARD OF TRUSTEES, LEFT, AND A LOCAL OFFICIAL PARTICIPATE IN A RIBBON-CUTTING EVENT FOR THE JOHN PAUL RIDDLE STUDENT CENTER IN JULY OF 1975.

Previous page: A VIEW OF THE FLIGHT LINE IN THE MID-1970S.

Progress continued as Embry-Riddle broke ground for a new aviation maintenance training facility, flight center, dormitories, administration building, and library. A stainless steel sculpture replicating the Wright brothers' first flight at Kitty Hawk was erected in front of the new library. It has become a landmark and popular backdrop for photos taken by students and alumni.

Photos clockwise from left: Gen. Bill Spruance, from left, Gen. Ken Tallman, John Paul Riddle, Jay Adams, and Eric Doten review architectural plans for Spruance Hall, which was built in 1987; Tine Davis and Gen. Bill Spruance converse after breaking ground for the Gill Robb Wilson Flight Center; Students relax in a dorm room in the 1980s.

Opposite page: Workers assemble the stainless steel replica of the Wright brothers' flyer in front of Hunt Library in October of 1989.

Previous page: Groundbreaking for the aviation maintenance center.

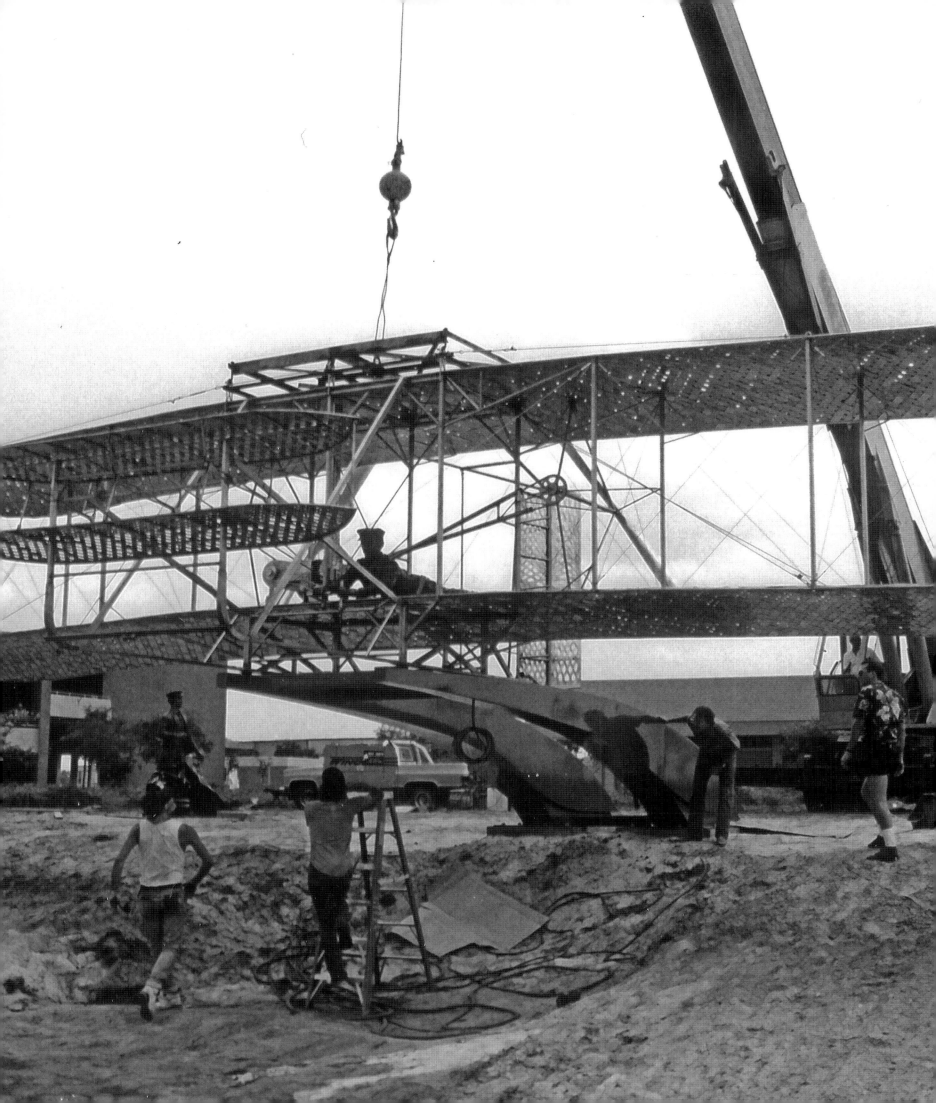

The campus in Prescott, Ariz., had been home to a small liberal arts college before Embry-Riddle acquired it in 1978. The campus weathered many challenges and fought to prove it could survive, leading to a major effort by the university to construct new buildings and improve existing facilities.

Photos clockwise from left: WILLIAM WALDOCK, PROFESSOR OF SAFETY SCIENCE, SPEAKS AT THE DEDICATION OF THE S. HARRY ROBERTSON CRASH INVESTIGATION LABORATORY, WHICH HE DIRECTS; STUDENTS LEARN TO INVESTIGATE AIRCRAFT ACCIDENTS IN PRESCOTT'S RENOWNED "CRASH LAB"; MEMBERS OF THE GOLDEN EAGLES FLIGHT TEAM POSE AFTER WINNING THE 1999 NATIONAL CHAMPIONSHIP AT THE SAFETY AND FLIGHT EVALUATION CONFERENCE SPONSORED EVERY YEAR BY THE NATIONAL INTERCOLLEGIATE FLYING ASSOCIATION. THE PRESCOTT TEAM HAS WON MORE NATIONAL SAFECON CHAMPIONSHIPS THAN ANY OTHER COLLEGE TEAM; JOHN PAUL RIDDLE REGALES STUDENTS WITH STORIES OF AVIATION HISTORY, IN WHICH HE PLAYED AN IMPORTANT PART, DURING A VISIT TO THE PRESCOTT CAMPUS.

Opposite page: JOHN PAUL RIDDLE LIVED TO SEE THE SCHOOL HE FOUNDED EXPAND FAR BEYOND HIS DREAMS. HERE, HE VISITS THE TINE AND EUNICE DAVIS LEARNING CENTER AT PRESCOTT, WHICH WAS DEDICATED IN 1979.

Previous page: AN AERIAL VIEW OF THE PRESCOTT CAMPUS.

Embry-Riddle in Prescott is a modern, thriving campus, renowned for its focus on aviation and aerospace education, including a unique degree program in global security and intelligence studies. It also boasts a multi-acre outdoor lab where students learn to investigate aircraft accidents by examining wreckage from actual plane crashes that were relocated to the site.

Above photos from left: EMBRY-RIDDLE PRESIDENT JACK HUNT VISITS WITH FACULTY MEMBERS AT THE PRESCOTT CAMPUS; PRESCOTT CAMPUS ALUMNUS SCOTT O'GRADY '89 RETURNS TO HIS ALMA MATER TO SPEAK WITH STUDENTS FOLLOWING HIS DRAMATIC SURVIVAL AND RESCUE IN BOSNIA AFTER HIS U.S. AIR FORCE JET WAS SHOT DOWN WHILE ENFORCING A NO-FLY ZONE THERE IN 1995.

Opposite page: THIS F104 STARFIGHTER, ACQUIRED FROM NASA, IS A WELL-KNOWN LANDMARK AT THE PRESCOTT CAMPUS.

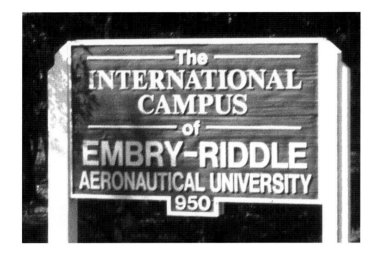

Embry-Riddle Worldwide began modestly in 1970, when Embry-Riddle first offered five aviation courses at Fort Rucker, Ala. The response from military aviators was overwhelming, prompting the university to establish additional centers of the "International Campus" at military bases around the United States, in England, and Germany. Today, Embry-Riddle Worldwide offers degree programs to working adults at more than 150 sites around the world, and through online study. Its coursework is delivered both in the classroom and through award-winning proprietary online technology that meets the higher education needs of students who are always on the go.

Above photos clockwise from left: IN ITS EARLY YEARS, EMBRY-RIDDLE WORLDWIDE UNDERWENT SEVERAL NAME CHANGES, INCLUDING INTERNATIONAL CAMPUS AND EXTENDED CAMPUS; STAFFERS AT THE NORFOLK, VA., EDUCATION CENTER PROUDLY BEAR THE EMBRY-RIDDLE FLAG; A GROUP OF NEW GRADUATES POSE AT THE HONOLULU CENTER.

Opposite page: JOHN PAUL RIDDLE PAID A VISIT TO STUDENTS TAKING EMBRY-RIDDLE COURSES AT A U.S. MILITARY BASE IN ENGLAND A FEW YEARS AFTER THE UNIVERSITY LAUNCHED ITS WORLDWIDE OUTREACH.

The Alumni Association was formed in 1966 by Embry-Riddle graduates seeking to maintain contact with each other. Eleven charter members registered the association as a nonprofit organization in Florida on March 14 of that year. Volunteer-operated through 1971, with only part-time support from various university staff, the association grew from 300 members in December 1967 to 3,200 in October 1970. In 1971, a new Alumni Association Constitution was approved, and a year later the university began officially dedicating paid staff to its operations. The first full-time director of Alumni Relations was hired in 1981. Today, the association has more than 100,000 members and is a strong presence on both residential campuses, with newly remodeled facilities providing a "home away from home" for graduates.

Photos clockwise from left: STUDENTS ENJOY VISITING IN THE OUTDOOR PATIO AREA NEAR THE DAYTONA BEACH ALUMNI ASSOCIATION OFFICE; FOREFRONT, LEFT TO RIGHT, DR. JOHN JOHNSON, UNIVERSITY PRESIDENT AND CEO, MICHELE BERG, EXECUTIVE DIRECTOR OF THE ALUMNI ASSOCIATION, AND DR. FRANK AYERS, EXECUTIVE VICE PRESIDENT AND CHIEF ACADEMIC OFFICER FOR PRESCOTT CAMPUS, CELEBRATE THE OPENING OF THE REMODELED ALUMNI ASSOCIATION OFFICES AT PRESCOTT; THE ALUMNI ASSOCIATION TEAM, PICTURED AT THE WRIGHT FLYER ON THE DAYTONA BEACH CAMPUS, COORDINATE ALUMNI CHAPTER/GROUP GATHERINGS ACROSS THE COUNTRY, HOST EVENTS THROUGHOUT THE YEAR AT POPULAR AIR SHOWS AND ON CAMPUS, AND PROVIDE VALUABLE COMMUNICATIONS TO KEEP ALUMNI CONNECTED.

Opposite page: THE NEWLY RENOVATED ALUMNI ASSOCIATION OFFICE AT PRESCOTT IS LOCATED IN THE HEART OF THE CAMPUS, FOSTERING STUDENT-ALUMNI CONNECTIONS AND PROMOTING AN ACTIVE STUDENT ALUMNI ASSOCIATION MEMBERSHIP.

Student organizations like the Student Alumni Association (SAA) also emerged during this time period. University records and photos indicate SAA clubs were established in the early 1970s at both the Daytona Beach and Prescott campuses. SAA fosters school spirit and pride, prepares students to become loyal alumni upon graduation, and creates connections between students and current alumni via networking and mentoring activities. In the early-2000s, SAA membership faltered and the club ceased to exist. Recognizing the value of such an organization for students, alumni and the university as a whole, the Alumni Association revived and re-launched the organization in 2010.

Photos clockwise from left: THE SAA CLUB SPONSORS SPEAKING ENGAGEMENTS AND OTHER ACTIVITIES ON CAMPUS. HERE, MEMBERS OF A 1970S-ERA CLUB POSE WITH THEIR GUESTS AT ONE SUCH EVENT; SAA MEMBERS VISIT WITH STUDENTS DURING A BBQ EVENT HELD OUTSIDE THE ALUMNI ASSOCIATION OFFICE; RETIRED AIR FORCE COL. MARK TILLMAN, FORMER CHIEF PILOT OF AIR FORCE ONE, VISITS WITH SAA MEMBERS DURING HIS VISIT TO DAYTONA BEACH IN 2011, IN HONOR OF VETERANS APPRECIATION DAY; SAA CLUB MEMBERS (CIRCA 1988-89) HOST A BOOTH AT A CLUB MEMBERSHIP DRIVE ON CAMPUS.

Opposite and following page: 2011 EMBRY-RIDDLE AERONAUTICAL UNIVERSITY GRADUATES CELEBRATE.